pauses
on the
path

pauses
on the
path

Idris Mears

First published 2022 by Lote Tree Press
www.lotetreepress.com

Paperback ISBN 978-1-7398271-8-2
Hardback ISBN 978-1-7398271-9-9

© Idris Mears 2022
All rights reserved

Designed by Maktaba
www.maktaba.co.uk

A CIP catalogue record for this book is available from the British Library

Cover image: fran_kie/Shutterstock.com

بسم الله الرحمن الرحيم

in the course of a lifetime
no two lords in one breast

contents

introduction	14
words to the giver	20
between Your hands	21
in the garden	22
guardian trees	23
a prayer	25
perfection	26
deeds	27
feat of clay	28
visions of the same	29
the ant's world	30
in the garden	32
the watches of the night	34
the watches of the night	35
celebration	36

night watch   37

the veil   39

the veil (2)   40

revelation   41

in plato's cave   42

plato's cave   43

space and time   44

the point   46

a perfect pain   47

contentment   48

the power of words   49

on my conscience   50

judgment day   52

stopping in cover   53

the bestiary of the heart and mind   54

tribe of adam   56

ruins   58

revolution   59

wisdom of the ages   62

prayer is a secluded brook — 64

times of finding — 65

submission — 70

the river of prayer — 72

hid in plain sight — 74

the prayer line — 75

stepping through to destiny — 76

on the edge — 78

belonging — 80

setting out — 81

the secret of be! — 82

the way of muhammad — 85

pulled by the moon — 86

ruled by the moon — 87

return to the ocean — 88

the pilgrim — 89

in the heartache of a dry season — 92

interim — 93

the silk road — 94

hope	95
return	96

waiting for the wave   98

waiting for the wave	99
adlestrop 2020	100
warning	102
syria and beyond	103
uae 2017	105
for the coming man	107
the axes of modernity	109
perdition	111

now it is autumn   112

the path	113
passing on	114
you have crossed	116
finding	117
in memoriam	118
sailing in alien waters	120
season of reflection	122
lost causes	123

death wish   124

in thanks   **126**

great saints   127

the prince   129

introduction

introduction

These poems have taken a long time to emerge. When young I wrote poetry, and if asked what I wanted to be would answer a poet. Then at university I fell in love with theatre and saw performance as an embodied poetry that transformed the being of the performer into a receptacle of meaning for the audience. This spiritual longing drove me to leave university, and what it represented of conforming to the conventions of a culture of dead information, and to strike out to find living knowledge. In a short space of time, I found myself at the feet of a teacher, Shaykh ʿAbdalQadir as-Sufi, in whom I saw the wisdom and gravity that I aspired to. He showed me that the door to being fully human was submission to the Real in a sane and balanced way, and that this was Sufism, the core of Islam, and that the flesh of the fruit was not attainable without the protection of the skin. Indeed, the zest and the perfume reside in the rind and the fruit is one indivisible whole.

Just by meeting him and recognising his spiritual reality I had already crossed the threshold of entering Islam, but it remained to formally pledge my commitment to 'five prayers a day and waiting for death'. I made this witnessing, or *shahadah,* at his hand in April 1973.

One of the great reliefs of becoming Muslim and the recognition that there was a Creator was that I no longer had to define myself to myself and to the world as being creative. In celebration of this freedom, shortly after my *shahadah*, I went to my parents' house where my possessions were in storage and made a bonfire of my poems and paintings.

pauses on the path

Many adventures and 'meetings with remarkable men' ensued in the following twenty years without me needing to put anything on paper, but in Ramadan in 1993 I performed i'tikaf, spiritual retreat, in the Ihsan Mosque in Norwich. After a sublime night, which I am sure was the Night of Power that Muslims look for in each year that the Qur'an promises is better than a thousand months, I noticed, sat wrapped in my cloak in the emerging light, beads of dew bejewelling each leaf on the tree outside the window in resonance with the gleam from my prayer beads. Later that day I was compelled to write this short poem:

in the texture of dawn's soft wrap
each glistening bead tells
its glory tale
of night's drenching

It now forms part of the poem, 'times of finding'. Its marriage of inner and outer, of meaning and sensory, in a tangible image remains the essence of what I try to achieve in poetry. Poetic technique and language are flourishes that add impact, for instance in the way that 'tells' in these lines relates both to telling a story and telling beads.

There are also references in the poems that Muslims will pick up on, like the use of the word 'glory'. This echoes the expression *subḥānallāh*, Glory be to God and the root relates to swimming - 'drenching' in water, and sounds similar to *ṣubḥ*, or dawn prayer. However, I am consciously trying in my poetry not to define myself as a 'Muslim' poet, and consciously trying to connect a general readership to the universal experience of being human and having a path. But, as I am steeped in them, I inevitably use Islamic imagery, values and thought. I hope they don't get in the way and rather that they show a way.

More poems have emerged sporadically after this initial foray, but I haven't made writing poetry a daily discipline, so I don't know if I have fulfilled the criteria of Malcolm Gladwell that the key to achieving expertise in any skill is to practise it correctly for 10,000 hours. The reflection that poetry should rest on I have practised, and I have been immersed in books and words all my life. There are however three people to whom I am indebted, who in their own creative practice have certainly surpassed this limit. Two I have dedicated poems to: Daniel 'Abdal-Hayy Moore, the poet, and John Mu'adh Kingerlee, the painter. The third is Joel Yusuf Hayward who has encouraged me to believe that I may have a genuine voice. I thank him for his friendship and support, and for acting as a sounding post in recent years.

This leaves me to acknowledge and thank people who have been central to my life for a long and eventful time: Shaykh ʿAbdalQadir as-Sufi for his guidance and Shaykh ʿAbdalHaqq Bewley for his companionship. I would also be neglectful not to mention companions and mentors who have gone ahead of me on this path and returned to their Lord: Hajj ʿAbdalʿAziz Redpath, Hajj ʿAbdalHamid Evans, Hajj ʿAbdalHalim Orr, Sidi Ibrahim Thompson, Hajj Abdallah Powell, Imam Salihu Djabbi and Sidi Mustafa McDermott. They are present in the poems.

pauses on the path

Last and certainly not least, I thank my wife, Hajjah Mansurah Mears, for her support in all ways, and my children and grandchildren for simply being themselves.

words to the Giver

words to the Giver

between Your hands

words fail in face of Your Face
yet powerless and shamefaced
with the power of words You have gifted me
i give words to the Giver beyond the given
and plunge into the pool of dappled light
between the cupped palms of the pleader

o You! we live between Your caring hands
and it is only our calloused and careless shape
that makes for roughness in the holding

so You! efface us with the musk of the perfumer's hands

all that is held in musk is suffused by musk

in the garden

in the garden

for Hajj ʿAbdalHamid Evans
guardian trees

whether the tree was planted

and staked with intention

or whether it was a wild sapling

destiny pushed through

the undergrowth of the norwich cemetery

i don't know

but God knew and God knows

the branches spread a shade

of peace over my companions

and God knows us each

and our resting places

and i hope to lie under it too

or under another of the guardian

trees of paradise

in paris or constantia or abu ayyub

or on the mountain top

under the cork oak beside the great qutb

trees watered by the mercy of centuries

as in my short time i have been rained on

by the blessing of the water

i drank at the breaking of the fast

pauses on the path

the joy of the water i swam in

the cleansing of the water

i used to prepare for prayer

and in course the water used

to wash me for the grave

in the garden

a prayer

in the garden today
i was working for a robin
digging up his lunch of worms
a busy version of the lazing hippopotamus
whose body heat draws insects for his attendant bird
but usually i am just working
in my wasteful human way
for the rats
and in the long run
for the worms
- so much for my industry and utility

but i pray i found
in the stillness and joy
of my work-honed reflection
a moment of sanity
between the madness of losing meaning
and the madness of imposing it

perfection

just as plants need the right
soil and water and light
and the right testing
of frost and drought
the age of the perfectly nurtured
body in the perfect garden
is thirty-three
when the glow of youth
meets settled maturity
and until we reach the age of forty
we don't have the fortitude to be
perfectly at ease with ourselves
and white hairs at sixty give us
dignity without airs
and if not perfectly stupid
we start to be a little bit wise
and at eighty all that is forgivable is forgiven
and the age of the perfected soul
is whatever time it takes
to face death with no regrets

in the garden

deeds

as with the carpet on the loom
for the weaver and the fly that settles
for the eternity of a moment on its weft
with weeds it is a matter of perspective

in my war to stop them colonising my garden
i keep sight of their advance from the insubstantial
whose roots hardly nibble at the crust of the soil
but give cover to the pernicious spreaders and deep rooters
and the tenacious treelings growing implacably in their
own tree time

against my will to impose order in my garden
these terrorists are only freedom fighters reclaiming
conquered land

in the ebb and flow of the battleground
both friend and foe advance in the same ranks and with
the same tactics

so my fellow garden tenders attend to small deeds

feat of clay

i broke my back today
shovelling a trench in clay
and now i know what clods
we sons of adam are

lumpy and cloying
as common as muck
stuck in the mud sods
resisting the workman's spade,
weighed down with the elemental
rain that won't drain away,
clinging to the soles
with a dead hand

needing artisan hands
to knead us on the slab
shape us on the wheel
anoint us with glaze
fire us in the kiln
make us useful
maybe even
beautiful

in the garden

visions of the same

do we but live in versions
of the same dreams
so do you too return to a clearing
in clear winter light
and through the tracery of winter trees
see a track up the slope of dead bracken
to the flint wall of the great estate
and know that if you were to set off
there is a small gate with the latch left off
somewhere along its length
and beyond it exquisite and unbounded
an early summer garden endlessly fresh after rain
and in your yearning can you all but smell
the alchemy of its fragrances
all but feel the gentle breeze
all but see the shaken silver of the poplar trees
all but hear the rustle of each leaf
be all but embraced by its utter ease

the ant's world

bowling along the lanes of a landscape sculpted
by generations of human use and neglect
the windscreen of my life and times'
addiction to the auto-mobile
puts the 'screen' between
me and the eye-
smarting sweet reek of the bonfire
the shoulder-hunching bluster of the wind bowling
the bone-dry leaves along

in this remove of movement
eyes extract each detail
that poplar with those storm-weathered pennants in its rigging
that wisp of smoke dark cat on its morning patrol
padding with intent through the overgrowth of the dew-silvered verge
that face of a child pressed like a prisoner
to the window of a car passing
into that exact future

in the garden

i like a wild-eyed vagrant
stuffing scraps of paper into the pockets and
sleeves of a tattered coat
for later reference
or to pass on to some ragamuffin
who tags alongside for a while
in the companionship of the road
in hope that on one scrunched scrap
there is a glimpse of a secret
name signifying
something

oh to stop
and press brow into cold damp grass
smell the chill of the earth
still the heart and cool the eye
in the ants' and other worlds

in the garden

i hope that if i am honored

with the garden of ease

i won't lounge all day

on a silken couch

but have vital hands in loamy soil

with sun on a supple back

feeling no nagging distraction

from an uneasy self

or run free as an innocent boy

chasing friends through the bushes

in the expanse of child time

and retire to bed

enjoying being

properly tired out

the watches of the night

the watches of the night

o Beloved!
Your troops have overrun
the defences of my heart
and chased sleep from the field

my petty loves are banished
from Your conquered realm
and i patrol the borders of my soul
in the watches of the night
to guard against their sneaking back

may my paces in the dark be counted

celebration

poets and philosophers
dowsers and potholers
each in their way
track the underground
stream in our dreams

journeys at night
unite the shores
we are between

surely we come from Allah
and surely to Him we return

so let us celebrate
the diamonds exploding like starbursts
from the beaten metal of the sea's skin
and the froth of the breakers
more dear than stuff

the watches of the night

night watch

once again you find yourself
entombed in the dark house
feeling your way
in the dead air of the stairwell
footfall deadened by dust
no light but a chink
of moonlight seeping
from beneath the furthest door
on the furthest landing

you recall the child's
first aloneness
in the night garden
heart alive with dread and daring
mystery in the familiar
familiarity in the mysterious

in the room beyond the door you know
the window is open to the vast
inkwell of the night sky
a night breeze rustling the curtains

pauses on the path

the scuttling of a mouse across the floorboards

the fluttering of a moth's wings

the humming of the starlight

the scratching of the nib on the page

the veil

the veil
is a one-way mirror

on the side beyond
the observation room

on the near side
the naked bulb
witnesses you
and your reflection
and the recording
of the interrogation

so if you want to see
unseen presences
switch off the light
stop the tape
and in the dark
the mirror will dim

and stars gleam
through the screen

the veil (2)

no matter how clear

the mirror

the image is reversed

we don't see ourselves

until we rise out of the body

and witness the empty shell

of the sleeper

or the corpse laid out

revelation

he is there

just ahead of me

as i follow discreetly

picking a night path

by the light

of the expanding heavens

up through the scree

to the mouth of the cave

and in my standing there

i am aware

within

the echoing word

has been spoken

that subsists

persists

in the held breath

of before before

and after after

in plato's cave

plato's cave

man lives in caves

savoring the ancient aromas

of the garden shed

weighing a lifetime

in books

read and unread

on a groaning shelf

lingering in an open field

bathed in the last light

of a full June day

spent in company

and yet solitary

in plato's cave

space and time

one Moroccan afternoon
in the cool of the saint's tomb
i took tea with my companions
among them the holy fool

i was eager to drink in
the light of his face
and watched him closely
beyond what decorum permits
as he was absorbed in the elsewhere

a shaft of sunlight caught his glass
and the amber liquid in it
as he lifted it to his lips
and he kept the glass there
poised at the tipping point
playing with the radiant drop

he is playing with space and time
it is not correct to watch
his drunkenness will overwhelm me

in plato's cave

i will be the fly in the amber
i told myself and lowered my eyes
for a humbled moment
before curiosity overpowered
my good sense and manners
and looking up he was gone
sitting twenty impossible feet away
up close to the tomb

the question is
whose moment was expanded
mine or his?

the point

if these sons of puritans ask
what is the point of life
meaning their task in life
point out that life is not a hook
to hang your tattered coat on
with its pinned medals
its stuffed pockets
its scuffs and stains and patches

but you do exist
and there is no
exit strategy
so be by that Being
empty and thankful

and isn't that the point
or at least a point
to begin and end with

in plato's cave

a perfect pain

jesus and his companions
on a road to meet the world
come across the carcass of a dog

how foul, the disciples say
how bright its teeth, jesus replies

today i am as jesus at peace
or at least not at war with Perfection
perfect the sacred geometry
of bird prints on the sand
perfect the immanence
of cloud formations
perfect the scruffy elegance
of the acacia trees
perfect the strewn trash
laid with precision
as if it were on tracey emin's bed
perfect the ugliness and pain that dog us
let alone the perfect slights and irritations

contentment

in blessed distress
we remember
the mercy of light and air
and the ground we stand on
is shared alike
by fortunate and bereft

contentment is
not being distraught
not being knocked off
the straight thought
from the centered point
by a stray wind

there is no shelter from the storm
contentment is not
the lull of a charmed life
the blessed seek
the company
of the distressed

the power of words

the heart
turns on words
a word in the ear that warns
a word in the ear that warms
or a word in the ear that worms

a man they say
is as good as his word
a word to keep and a bed to lie on
a word before sleep and a bed to rise from
a word on the death bed that can be relied on

i say the word is the greatest weapon
the word of truth
in the face of a tyrant

yet the greatest word of all
is the word from beyond
the heart of silence

on my conscience

i confirm
the Book and the Man
when i say
i don't need any book
or man to tell me
by hook or by crook
i steal time from Time
so how can the heart
overlook less subtle crime

the thieving cat
crouches in the corner
challenging the room
with his loot
but laps milk
from the bowl
without looking up

do we think
we can chance our luck
(as if we could)

in plato's cave

and throw a challenge
in His face and not face
the hollow ache in that place
where He is known
and not dread what follows
in the following place

judgment day

one part of me
(not an easy one to put away)
waits for judgment day
as a final tribunal
whose arbitrator will resolve
every grievance in my favour
but that feels to another part
(and not an easy one to make stay)
like a continuation of hell
and this better judge longs to drink
a cleansing draught that clears
the breast of vindication
and vindictiveness

stopping in cover

the settlers
not quite settled on the land
and not quite in the know
say with god-given conviction
flightless bird-brained ostriches
take flight by burying
their heads in the sand

maybe say the bird-trained bushmen
who know the lie of the land
they are just checking
their hidden eggs and chicks
before they run to ground
and we all know whose wisdom
is passed over
and whose is passed around

so God knows you passers-by
if you spy me stopping in cover
pressing my forehead on the ground
i am not fleeing from the cares of life
but facing them full-on

the bestiary of the heart and mind

ecologists and other denizens
of the environment of fact
have no words for the habitat
where the thought fox skirts
the edge of the wood
a presence known
by stink and scat and tracks
and the momentary sight
in the covert of a slight
twitch of snout and whiskers
and the challenge of bold eyes

the media machine
desperately seeking
sends trampling teams
into what should remain
impassable terrains
to document the private life
of species doomed before
and now yet more
by the camera's eye

in plato's cave

and blithely passes by

the forest where

creatures of rarer meaning

have their lairs

in the bestiary

of the heart and mind

pauses on the path

tribe of adam

tribe of adam noble
not brute near beast near mute

language not hacked from grunts
but deep singing bursting whole
and clear like a skylark's hymn
from the bell cavity of breasts
with beating hearts

greeting the other
with the grammar of respect
and intimacy
not the leveller's savage text
to unitary citizen or avatar ambivalent

three hundred words
for the colours and gaits of horses
not the blunt three hundred words
of internationalese

not cowed ignoramus

in plato's cave

holding totems and formulas

against the darkness beyond the firelight

or draining the bowl

to the dregs of emptiness

in the penthouse or the gutter

but the leaping of archer mind

naming the constellations

and hallowing the dawn and the dusk

with awe and worship

not quick-witted ape testing the limits

baring bum and fangs in one-upmanship

or strutting its stuff

on the catwalk or the trading floor

but the unconditional generosity

of the physician who does not flee the plague

but treads the modest path

of restraint and kindliness

ruins

surely man is in loss

ruins pull on us
with eloquence and elegance
peeled of their human makeup and gloss
nature primps them subtly with lichen and moss
weathers them in grave kind
and from the still pool of their silence
well up deeper voices than the this
and that chitchat of occupation
just so we lost blighters find
unravelling tales of blighted lives
more gripping and more resonant
than the laboured construct
of worthiness
so human what
a tragic loss

revolution

within the continuum of hurtle and spin
tectonic plates inch close or slip apart
until lurch liquefies the claimed ground
or wrench releases the weight of magma
to overwhelm the common place

so with the self
so here in the city
at the heart of the world
they say
we never saw it coming

except for the watchman
in the winds and clear air
of his high place
true eye trained
on the patchwork plain

and the cultivator made patient
by weather and the seasons
bent to the dark soil
waiting for the ash to settle

cars passing in the night

the you in the dream
is driving alone
shore to shore
on a highway across the great plain
pushing through the curtain
of a starless night
nothing in sight
but red tails and white brights
each vehicle funnelling a sole traveller
into a future of dark shapes
sighted just beyond
the reach of the beam
and in the rear view
the past is swallowed
by darkness

somewhere on the journey
the lights and signs of a rest area
pull you in for gas and a burger
and some banter with the server
but you do not linger

in plato's cave

you are only passing through

and then you recall
you have passed through here before
and there is something important
you need to say
or valuable you have misplaced
that makes you anxious
and you must not leave
this place or this dream
without remembering
what it is

but though you resist
you wake with an itch
at the edge of memory

wisdom of the ages

i would be blessed in life
with the wisdom of the ages
and knowledge of the hour
if i but knew how string
such a simple single line
got tangled up in knots
just lying on the floor
or waiting in a drawer
for me
to waste hours of my time
and my peace of mind
unravelling it

prayer is a secluded brook

times of finding

in the heart's seeing
between lost and forgotten
and yet to be
and never to be
found are found
lifetimes and stopping
places of prayer
and finding

   1. dusk

at the margin of day
with day's eve
the alongside world
nudges up like a cat
aloof but familiar
gathering in dusky shades
the palette behind lids closed
against the light
of a window opening
beyond

pauses on the path

2. night

on the mirror black
night sea face between
countless stars
fathomless deeps
night sailor teases out the slack
alert in repose
watching for signs of wind
and then the stir of breeze before dawn
and sense stiffened he hauls
into the centre and holds
there for that
moment's catch of breath

3. dawn

in the texture of dawn's soft wrap
each glistening bead tells
its glory tale
of night's drenching

prayer is a secluded brook

    4. noon

at dead of noon
frowning angels
dance on the wall of heat
and all creatures shroud from the blast

depth falls away from vision
and only stirs the play of silver
on sheeny faces

in white room body laid out
the heart within without
all these surfaces all these appearances

    5. afternoon

in the late afternoon
as the last light is squeezed
from the Painter's tube
adrift with the throng
in antique city heart
weary with usage

pauses on the path

you furrow a path
past the wares of man
stacked up bolts of satin
and shoddy and taffeta
bold brass rank upon rank
rank odours covered over
stratum upon stratum
abstracts of sound woven
into declensions of rhythm and cadence
ever-changing in their sameness
moom-moo baa-paa nee-nee nah-nah
and then you slip
from the press of the heedless
and pass through the portal
heart lifted into the stillness
of the forecourt's glade
of lengthening shade
and the archways
of the inner chamber
beckon into hallowed space
and heart illumined
you part a way through
the thick air between

prayer is a secluded brook

the forest of pillars

of a lamp-lit grove

and take your place next

a cloaked form

to wait the call

and the form turns

with a swish of his mantle

and greets you with peace

and a waft of mountain herb

you stumbled across

in a secret recess

after morning rain

submission

the swimmer said
i learnt to swim before i was two
and the memory of taking to water
is written on the ripples
of the waters of the womb
and leaves no mark on the tablet
i heave around to give my me solidity

so in water i am
submerged in the elemental
narrative suspended
in complete submission

the seer said
water is everywhere
and prayer is a secluded brook
flowing in the thicket
that borders the path

the pilgrim can bow his head
and brush through

prayer is a secluded brook

the nettles and thorns
and enter with a lift of the head
and an inrush of the musk of stream
a chapel of green and dappled light
alive with water plants and water life
and water dancing in delight

the river of prayer

you say
when you pray
you feel the lack
of you feeling

but who is this you
you are at such pains
to feel should be there?

The Real really
doesn't care
or judge you
for what you feel

don't you see
you make you
The Royal We

listen
with a listening heart
to the oft-repeated

prayer is a secluded brook

you are not the possessor
of the case
He is the King
of judgment day

prayer is a river
that washes you away

be in its stream of sound
whether soft or loud

listen
and drown

hid in plain sight

hot eyed
heartless masters
of all we survey
reckon and measure
we glare at the screen
of there-ness
where-ness?
scaring the angels away
and in plain sight
He hides

but in the slave's
lowered gaze
when we let our focus
narrow and glaze
and the heart rises
and the salve of prayer
cools our eyes
we are aware
in the here-ness
He sees us

the prayer line

the prayer line
is a stand of trees
the roots outreach the canopy
and speak a tongue
of deeper connectivity
than sighing boughs
and rustling leaves

o Allah keep me
in that company
we stand up straight
but on the night of power
prostrate
completely

stepping through to destiny

a saint may have prayed for me, an expatriate child, growing up in Bahrain

the glance

by chance
may some man of God
have seen you
child of the book
making your way
through the souk
and blessed you
with a glance

chance is in the hands of God
fairly dispensed
with or without
grace and favour

so o man of blessing
favour with a look
every fair and graceful child
who crosses your path
whose look you favour

an incident whilst hitchhiking along the Dalmatian Coast in 1971

on the edge

fleeing the city
finding himself
on the brink of a cliff
the young brave visions a perfect arc
a hundred and fifty foot of free flight
into the advancing weight of wave

he sees in his embrace of the air
he will soar forever beyond
all dreads and evasions and lack of maturing
he will secure courage and purpose
he will be a warrior

and having seen his victory
to retreat from this meeting place with himself
without committing the glorious dreadful dive
in the face of the advancing years
would be more dreadful

stepping through to destiny

so three stretched seconds of clench and brace
and the concrete embrace of the sea later
he finds life cannot be mastered
with one leap

courage must be found
at every edge and on every cliff

pauses on the path

In December 1972, invited to a 'public meeting', I found myself in a gathering of dhikr

belonging

for seekers all times are strange
and we converge at the door
of witnessing in strange ways
each in his own time and circumstance
with his own route through the medina's maze
of passages and blind alleys
i for one approached in the gloom
of gathering dusk
and stumbled across the threshold
into dazing light
and in that moment of blind remove
found myself in the room
at peace sensing the vastness
aware without turning
the door had closed on me
and the company
gathered in circles and closed ranks
in here belonging

stepping through to destiny

an aspiring actor, after that night of dhikr, my first meeting with Shaykh ʿAbdalQadir as-Sufi

setting out

all the world's a stage

who the seer said as he read the actor's lines
is looking at you up there on the stage
from the void beyond the footlight's glare

and under his gaze the staged answers
took fright and left exit right
leaving him on the bare boards
with the eyes of the parents as company

he took his hand or he took his
and said yes the whisky bottle
and the breast are best left
at the green room door
if you seek to see really
or really be seen

the secret of be!

the seeker said to the seer
there is a thing I do not see
why is it so easy to be
perfectly will-lessly
time and space and energy
so easy to be
a wheeling galaxy
with a dust cloud of a billion suns
a sun with orderly planets
held by gravity
a planet with a consort moon
so easy to be
an ocean with currents
and moon-pulled tides
a sea-pulled river seeking its course
across an alluvial plain
a peaty dark upland stream
so easy to be
an up-thrust mountain
a tumbling scree of rocks
a slope of grassy down

stepping through to destiny

decked with gorse and broom

a stand of pines keeping watch

on the brow of a hill

a sheltered valley of woods

and pastureland

a field of ripe wheat

a poppy in the hedgerow

so easy to be

an army of ants

a hive of bees

a colony of squawking gulls

a chorus of nightingales

so easy to be

a pride of deadbeat lions

submitted to the noonday heat

a stampede of panicked antelope

a family of chimpanzees

murderously on the prowl

so easy to be

a solitary wolf

intent on the sounds

and scents of the trail

so easy to be

pauses on the path

a cell a limb a body

even so easy to be

an urge a thought a sensibility

why so uniquely

hard to be

perfectly wilfully me

the seer replied

where there's a will

there's a way

give up this me

willingly

then you'll see

it was always

willed

to be

the way of muhammad

the denying 'me'
is pushed
along the path
of fate
by resentful ghosts
and affirming demons

the affirming 'I'
pulls revealing
angels onto the threshold
of moment
and steps through
to destiny

pulled by the moon

ruled by the moon

from above the trees
creatures of the air
see everywhere
glints of water
showing through seams and tears
as if the land were cast on the waters
like a rumpled jacket

these secretive places
pull like the moon
on our bodies of water
blood and secretion
earthed by flesh and bone

we make pilgrimages
to wells and streams
and at appointed times
set out for the great ocean

return to the ocean

for the timid
being intrepid
is to inch out of their depth
making sure of a watchful eye

valiant souls lose sight
of the shoreline
and seek aloneness
in a directionless
horizon of sea and sky
exposed to the creatures
of the deep beneath
the surface swell

like turtles they return to land
to bury eggs and depart
with a last beckoning look
or wash up like beached whales
drawing concerned hearts
to their singularity

the pilgrim

another year and here you are
setting out for the gathering place
a drop of sperm a clot of blood a lump of flesh
a gust of wind wrinkling the face of the pond
for a precise number of ripples
a not yet beached piece of flotsam
on the coming and going of the tide
a spatter on the dust releasing the smell of rain
a droplet among the droplets
each with its witnessing angels
in the rivulets brooks streams rivers
niles and amazons of pilgrim flow
from far and near terrains
meanderers across the plains
and torrents disgorging from every ravine
the gentle and the fierce
the calm black and the foaming white
and all complexions between
filling out throughout
the body of the land
like capillaries and veins

pauses on the path

engorged after quenching the fast

a flash flood churned by earnestness

a tidal force pulled by joy and gravity

and astral conjunction

along its singing course

to swirl its dervish whirl

(he is still, the world spins)

around the settling place

and join with the gush on gush

from the wellspring

beneath the emptied heart of the earth

and seven heavens above

in the heartache of a dry season

interim

in the heartache

of a dry season

veterans of hard campaigns

shelter behind shutters

oil their weapons and wait

for clouds to gather

and the bidden word to fall

like forgiving rain

easing to the filaments of the soil

and stirring the soul of the seeds

to release a jewelled brocade

of desert flowers

a shawl of heart's ease

and restoration

the silk road

remember
 - when stalled to wait and waste
in the dried-out heart
of a continent seared
by heat and plagued
by dust devils
wrung air leaching the body
of its distant ocean moisture
leaving a rime of sweat and tears
and the liver's parched ache
for the return of rain –
the setting out
in the clement embrace
of a silken dawn

in the heartache of a dry season

hope

i pray the darkling heart

may sing still and summon

the will for joy when

sat by a window

on some desultory morn

at the boot end of the year

at the boot end of time

looking out on the years

and the ground down town

debris of the night past

and hopes trashed

strewn by a sour wind

a memory of the memory

of spring

is reflected in the glass

return

the grand apartment
has been shut up
for year on dreary year
and dust has settled
on the furniture and floors
and the mirrors are flecked
with tarnish

but now lord wastrel
has returned
from wandering
and it is time to recall
those honest and faithful retainers
to resume their daily chores

get care the maid
to open the windows
and let in the air
whisk away the cobwebs
with her feather duster
take off the dust covers

in the heartache of a dry season

get down on hands and knees
to scrub the marble tiles

get diligence the concierge
to sweep the stairs
with his trusty broom

get remembrance the cook
to lovingly prepare
nourishing fare
to put flesh on the frame
and vigour in the veins

get fortitude the butler
to fetch the vintage port
to revive the spirits

the lord has returned
send hope the footman
to summon lady joy

waiting for the wave

waiting for the wave

in the dream
i am on a cliff
at the edge of the world
watching the pacific rollers
crash against the rocks
and beside me my father
or it could be my teacher
or the presence
of all preceding generations
and then the ocean recedes
and the naked seabed
is littered with writhing
fish drowning in air
and we are waiting
for the great wave to arrive

i wake up and i am waiting
we are waiting
waiting for the wave

adlestrop 2020

a summer afternoon
over a hundred years ago
before my father was born
a young poet in uniform is on a branch line train
passing through the heart of his homeland

abroad the great war is changing the world
empires are falling and rising

the train stops at a country station
no one gets on or off
through the clouds of steam
he notes the name
adlestrop
and the train sets off again

drowsy from the sun and the clacking of the track
in reverie he revisits the bare platform
with its tended flowerbeds
and wildflowers beyond the picket fence
and hears a solitary blackbird

waiting for the wave

and imagines its song
as a stone dropped in a pond
rippling a chorus of connection
across the familiar land

he tenderly reflects on the homely
and inconsequential

the poet is killed on a foreign field
the poem visits again and again
like the wind of a passing train
shuddering the stationary carriage
making it seem you are moving
and it stood still

but after a long century's cycle
with pestilence abroad in the land
and the homely blighted
empires are rising and falling
and the great reckoning is nigh

warning

the minarets of this dust-blown city
peg down an awning of protection
but the groaning of the guy ropes
and the flapping of the rents
worry the rest of the wakeful
and the dead
and i have made my bed
and cannot lift a finger
in anger or in mourning
and no sound comes out
when i shout in warning
i can only turn over and supplicate
for the sleep of the dead
and while i wait
turn poems over in my head

syria and beyond

facing the devastation
of these ancient cities
it is callous not to grieve
the human cost
not to weigh the worth
of each human soul

in extremis
the good and the wicked
and the muddling through
each has a story
each a reckoning
each a face on a billboard
in our still standing city
saying is this us?

but as all turns to dust
dry historians know
dynasties ebb and flow
and some dry up leaving
in finality

pauses on the path

on the cracked bed
of an aral sea
wrecks of grand schemes
and ordinariness

so as I survey the cracks
on this city's facade
and vision the buildings
as hulks of mangled wire
and smashed concrete
an industrial artscape
sculpted by industrial war
i am dispassionately assessing
whether beneath there may be
the wells and cisterns
of continuity

uae 2017

as the cities hum
with directionless activity
and the drums of war murmur
like the ignored first twinges
of a heart attack
do these sons of navigators
of sand and sea
who paid no rent or tax
only the customary dues
of religion and trade
who lived by craft and graft and guile
and gathered news
from spoor and track
and cloud formation
and the intelligence
of the campfire shared
with the honoured guest
or the relative at the port of call
not see how they are rowing their ship
into the whirlpool
ears sealed with the wax

pauses on the path

of fat cat pensions and salaries

their captains strapped to the mast

maddened by the siren call

of being men of their time

for the coming man

on the platform
and in the forum
you air your niceties
and professions of piety
but the bereft
and the soon to leave
like me
are left in the air
between your words
and their needs

are you on the traces
of the mercy to all
or just po-faced faces
in a hall of mirrors
poring and bickering
over minutiae
with your own reflections
whilst history passes by

the unbecoming alpha male

pauses on the path

of the pretentious up-comers
has become the professional
scholar in the pocket
of whoever or whatever pays
a gravy spot to be flicked off
the cuff of the oligarch
leaving the faintest of stains

the coming prince will flay you
and reveal beneath the skin
what is real
or not

the axes of modernity

on the coromandel coast in kilakarai
on the monsoon route to china
i visited the saint who brought islam
and died in this baraka-drenched place
within decades of mustafa's passing

a baobab tree
brought with care from africa
and planted for shelter
had grown and engulfed his grave
and lent the site
the magic of God's beauty
beloved by the visitors
to the beloved saint
whose baraka grew
in the way that trees
and places of pilgrimage do.

but what I saw
entering the enclosure
was the rubble of the headstone

pauses on the path

the mighty tree had grown over
in an achingly empty charred space

petro-dollar remittance zealots
had descended on the grove
and hacked down the tree
with the axes of modernity
it took them a week
and then they burnt it
as an offering
to their fixed little idea of deity

the stony-hearted bigots
hadn't even distributed it as firewood

perdition

in the still hall

housing the heart

the weight of each beat

pushes the minute

hand of the grandfather

clock towards the chiming hour

yet still i am here

on a mall trawl with the troglodytes

(when did they last see the light)

every selfie a click closer

to perdition

now it is autumn

the path

on a hard day's tramp
along the coastal way
i pause to catch breath
hunkered in the shelter
of a hollow between the dunes
with the autumn sun on my face
and reflect on how this path
tracks a struggle
between land and sea
like the conflicting voices
of the heart

stretches where cliffs fall into the sea
and the bells of lost towns are heard
stretches where dunes succumb
to marram grass and the farmer's grasp

and always the journey winds on
relentlessly between
being built up
and being washed away

passing on

i have inherited my father's frame
and his way of holding himself
if not his way of holding the world
and when he died
i retrieved this coat from his closet
more than twenty years old
bought when he was sixty
and in perfect condition
- he always chose quality
and schooled by thrift
and the decency of hard times
cherished his possessions
as heirlooms to ward off penury

and i have felt comfortable in it
made it familiar by seven years'
hard-wear disregard and affection
the blithe generosity of softer times
but now i too am sixty
and with winter coming on
taking stock and inventory

now it is autumn

i am minded to pass it on
- after a generation's span
there is still life in it -
for someone else to assume

attires assumed and cast off
with the turn of the seasons
these fresh fall mornings remind me
of new school years a lifetime ago
and journeys to be embarked on
summer lingering in the bones
chill in the nostrils
warm breath on cold air
shaman's emanation
portending the coming
of frozen ground

pauses on the path

for Daniel 'Abdal Hayy Moore

you have crossed

they saw

an ecstatic wind-catcher

dancing entrancingly

at the prow of a longship

breasting the waves of the cosmic ocean

hurling warrior words

pell-mell into the wall

of the astral wind

i saw

a wily magpie pilgrim

dropping bright word

by bright word

patiently into the pit

to build a bridge

either way

you have crossed

now it is autumn

for Mu'adh John Kingerlee

finding

the great man the artist

forty years of application

layer upon layer

and still to be discovered

draws me into his world

as we pick a way through

the alleys of the old moorish quarter

revealing to me

in the weathering and defacing

layering and peeling

what his heart in hiding discerns

- the whirr of a bird breaking cover -

showing me finding

is training the heart to see

in memoriam

the party has washed up on the shores of dawn
and only we lingerers and early risers
are out at first light
combing for amber on the shining strand
sand hard packed by the weight
of the receded ocean
pebbles gleaming like gems
yet to be dulled
by the march of the day

between the tidelines
a marcher kingdom is revealed
exposed to the night chilled air
and the stabbing beaks of waders and gulls
savants of where to pick the bounty
concealed beneath the surface

in the night on the high tide
two more of our boon companions
the heart-stirrer shanty singer
the spirit-rouser hornpipe dancer

now it is autumn

rowed off in a skiff to the holding ship

moored out beyond

the curvature of the earth

now and then we spy on our horizon

the bobbing white flag of its topsail

a noah's ark of ones of a kind

at peace with the sea and themselves

the learned navigator

the diligent log keeper

the resolute bosun

the stalwart mate

the kindly surgeon

the reformed pirate

the dear ship's boy

and the exemplary captain we long to meet

sailing in alien waters

when i come again to home haven
after a lifetime of sailing in alien waters
under a flag of convenience
who will be waiting quayside
to recognise and welcome
the return of the tender child
inside this salt-cured hide

as i step from the plank onto the dock
i will seek out the faces of near ones
and dear companions
those noble souls of fair passage
on the trade winds
and battles around the horn
and the heartache of wait in the doldrums
and others not yet met
but celebrated in seafarers' yarns
living charmed lives
though life at sea is always hardship

and once on firm and lasting ground

now it is autumn

i will seek out a mountain tarn

to wash the salt away

and a summer meadow

to lie on to dry on

with the scent of drying grass

and the hum of angel wings

season of reflection

autumn's sweet light

reveals the shape of leaves

and colors of bark

summer has concealed

and as the sap recedes

to the dark soil

that seeks our rest

we take cheer in winter comforts

and wait for year's end

lost causes

the traveller's final footstep
lifts free from the last
grain of sand
and by the resolve of hope
sets out
to the saint of lost causes

the last crinkle of leaf
clings to the twig
held by the last molecule
of the sap of hope
and calls out
to the God of Lost Causes

death wish

i have a wish

when i take my final breath
may it be a birth
witnessed by children
who hold me
in the same gaze of joy
that spilled over
from the ocean
of my heart
when i first held them

may i do what it takes
to be that man
may they do what it takes
to be those people

in thanks

in thanks

two poems for Shaykh 'AbdalQadir as-Sufi

great saints

some say great saints
are mountains with beacons lit
beckoning the troops
and guiding the way
and when they fall
only rubble remains

better to say
they are mighty trees
who cleanse the world's air
and when they die
their stumps become havens
for fungi lichen mosses insects and birds

indeed they are already dead
when we think them alive
consumed by ivy that lovingly clings
reducing them to shapes
that were once beach oak or hornbeam

pauses on the path

saplings are nurtured

in the forest soil under their shade

and as Nature intended

take their place

or like the sycamore

the pods fly on the wind

and settle in the distance

even in cracks in tarmac and concrete

and see how implacably

butterfly besotting buddleias

rewild embankment ledges

and neglected city edges

no changing

God's doing in His creation

in thanks

the prince

no the seer said
i am not searching out
the mannerly prince with the common touch
well-fed well-scrubbed well-shod
well versed in the etiquette of the times
well prepared to take his appointed place
with his retinue and rents

no i keep my hopes on the horizon
waiting for the stranger from the wild places
with wildness in his heart
and strength in his sinews
tempered by test and task
bringing his band of dust-shod companions
who stand with him whatever the cost

i send out envoys to seek him
and ask after him from the travellers
spread the news of his coming
and prepare his place

pauses on the path

yes the seer said

he will come

he is searching for me

Also from Lote Tree Press

A Kaleidoscope of Stories:
Muslim Voices in Contemporary Poetry

Symphonies of Theophanies:
Moroccan Meditations
by Peter Dziedzic

All the Birds were Invited to a Feast in the Sky
by Soukeyna Osei-Bonsu

From this Street to the Moon
by Nabila Jameel

The Well at the Desert's Heart:
Verses of Healing
by Tony Bowland

Light Steps:
A Poem on the Seerah of Prophet Muhammad ﷺ
by Ali Scully

Peace Be Upon Us
by Iljas Baker

www.ingramcontent.com/pod-product-compliance
Lightning Source LLC
LaVergne TN
LVHW041640060526
838200LV00040B/1646